Better Homes and Gardens®

PASTA RECIPES

Our seal assures you that every recipe in *Pasta Recipes*
has been tested in the Better Homes and Gardens® Test Kitchen.
This means that each recipe is practical and reliable, and
meets our high standards of taste appeal.

For years, Better Homes and Gardens® Books has been a leader in publishing cook books. In *Pasta Recipes,* we've pulled together a delicious collection of recipes from several of our latest best-sellers. These no-fail recipes will make your cooking easier and more enjoyable.

Editor: Rosemary C. Hutchinson
Editorial Project Manager: Rosanne Weber Mattson
Graphic Designer: Harijs Priekulis
Electronic Text Processor: Paula Forest

On the front cover: Off-the-Shelf Italian Dinner
(see recipe, page 39)

Contents

All About Pasta

Derived from what is basically a flour and water mixture, pasta has long been associated primarily with Italian cuisine. This relationship probably began when Marco Polo introduced Italy to the noodle after his trip to China in the 1270's. However, there is evidence that ravioli was being eaten in Italy 20 years prior to Polo's travels.

Today, we are recognizing pasta's international appeal. The Germans delight in their spaetzle, the Chinese enjoy their wontons and eggrolls, and the Japanese savor their soba noodle. In this book, we focus on the many varieties of pasta there are to choose from and the variety of ways to use each pasta as an entrée, an accompaniment, a dessert, and a snack. The photos on the following pages will help you identify your pasta choices; the rest of the book will help you create something delicious.

Elbow Macaroni

Alphabets

Conchiglie

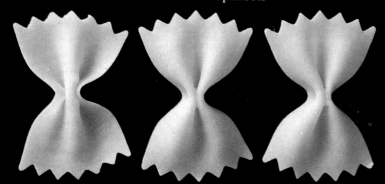
Farfalle

Orzo or Rosamarina

Rotelle

Cavatelli

Rigatoni

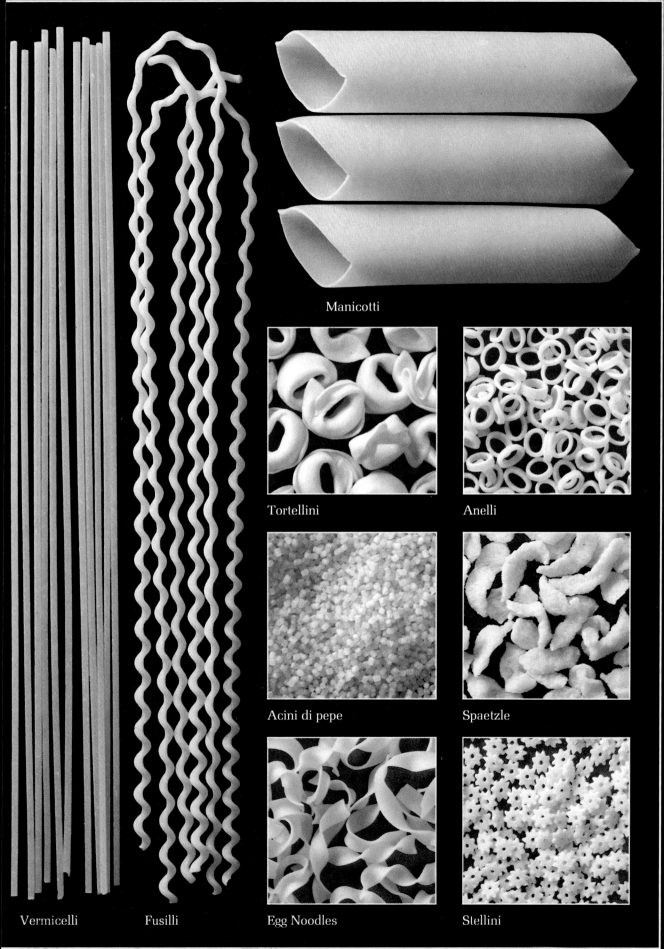

Manicotti

Tortellini

Anelli

Acini di pepe

Spaetzle

Vermicelli

Fusilli

Egg Noodles

Stellini

Ditalini

Tripolini

Nested Vermicelli

Mostaccioli

Lasagna

Ziti

Conchiglioni

Gemelli

Ravioli

Couscous

Rice Sticks

Ruote

Fettuccine

Mafalda

Egg Roll Wrapper

How to Make Pasta

Homemade Pasta

2⅓ cups all-purpose flour
½ teaspoon salt
2 beaten eggs
⅓ cup water
1 teaspoon olive oil
  or cooking oil

● In large mixing bowl stir together 2 *cups* of the flour and salt. Make a well in center.
● In a small mixing bowl combine eggs, water, and olive or cooking oil. Add egg mixture to flour mixture, then mix well.
● Sprinkle kneading surface with the remaining ⅓ cup flour. Turn dough out onto floured surface. Knead for 8 to 10 minutes or till smooth and elastic. Cover and let rest for 10 minutes.
● Divide dough into thirds. Roll dough (see below); cut and shape as desired (see drawings at right). Cook or store pasta as directed on page 10 or 14. Makes 1 pound fresh pasta.

Spinach Pasta

1 10-ounce package frozen chopped spinach, cooked and drained
2 eggs
1 teaspoon olive oil
  or cooking oil
2⅓ cups all-purpose flour
1 cup whole wheat flour
½ teaspoon salt

● Squeeze excess liquid from drained spinach. In a blender container or food processor bowl combine the spinach, eggs, and olive or cooking oil. Cover; blend or process till smooth.
● In a large mixing bowl stir together *2 cups* of the all-purpose flour, whole wheat flour, and salt. Make a well in center of the mixture. Add spinach mixture, then mix well.
● Sprinkle kneading surface with remaining ⅓ cup all-purpose flour. Turn dough out onto the surface. Knead for 8 to 10 minutes or till smooth and elastic. Cover; let rest for 10 minutes.
● Divide dough into thirds. Roll dough (see below); cut and shape as desired (see drawings at right). Cook or store pasta as directed on page 10 or 14. Makes 1½ pounds fresh pasta.

Rolling Directions

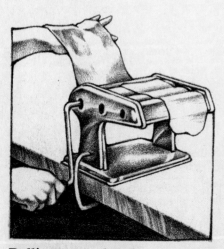
Rolling pasta dough.

Rolling pin method: Divide dough into thirds. On lightly floured surface roll each third into a ¹⁄₁₆-inch-thick rectangle of about 16x12 inches.
Pasta machine method: Divide dough into thirds. Pass dough through the pasta machine at its widest roller opening. If necessary, repeat at same setting to smooth dough.
● Reset machine at the next narrower opening; pass dough through machine. Repeat at same setting till dough is smooth.
● Continue resetting machine at narrower openings and rolling dough till it is about ¹⁄₁₆ inch thick. As needed, dust dough with flour to prevent sticking. (For easier handling, divide dough as it lengthens from successive rollings.)

Cutting and Shaping Directions

Cutting fettuccine by hand.

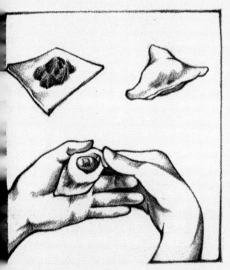

Filling and shaping cappelletti.

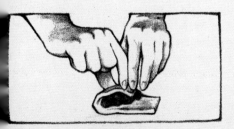

Shaping manicotti.

● After rolling dough, use a sharp knife or cutting blades on a pasta machine to cut dough as directed below for desired pasta.
● For filled pasta, use a desired filling from page 14 and shape pasta as directed below.

Linguine: After rolling dough, let it stand about 20 minutes to dry surface slightly. To cut dough by hand, roll it up loosely. Cut dough into ⅛-inch-wide slices. Lift and shake noodles to separate. *Or,* to cut dough using a pasta machine, pass dough through ⅛-inch-wide cutting blades. Then use a knife to cut noodles into desired lengths.

Fettuccine: After rolling dough, let it stand about 20 minutes. To cut dough by hand, roll it up loosely. Cut into ¼-inch-wide slices. Lift and shake noodles to separate. *Or,* to cut dough using a pasta machine, pass dough through ¼-inch-wide cutting blades. Then use a knife to cut noodles into desired lengths.

Mafalda: Using a fluted pastry wheel, cut dough into ¾-inch-wide strips. Cut noodles into desired lengths.

Lasagna: Using a sharp knife or fluted pastry wheel, cut dough into 2½-inch-wide strips. Cut noodles into desired lengths.

Cappelletti: Cut dough into 1½-inch squares. To stuff, place ¼ *teaspoon* filling on *each* square. Fold square into a triangle. Press edges together to seal. Place index finger against fold and bring the two outer corners of triangle together, pressing one corner over the other to seal. Repeat with remaining squares.

Tortellini: Using a 1½-inch round cutter, cut dough into circles. To stuff, place ¼ *teaspoon* filling on *each* circle. Fold circle in half. Press edges together to seal. Then continue shaping as directed for cappelletti (above). Repeat with remaining circles.

Ravioli: Using a sharp knife or fluted pastry wheel, cut dough into 1½- to 2-inch squares. To stuff, place *1 rounded teaspoon* filling on *each* square. Top with a second square. Press edges together with fork tines to seal. Repeat with remaining squares.

Cannelloni: Using a sharp knife, cut dough into 5x3½-inch rectangles. Cook as directed on page 10. Drain in a colander. Rinse with cold water, then drain again. To fill, place a rectangle with a short side toward you. Spoon about ⅓ *cup* filling across *each* rectangle just below center. Beginning at the bottom *edge,* roll pasta around filling. Repeat with remaining rectangles.

Manicotti: Using a sharp knife, cut dough into 5x3½-inch rectangles. Cook as directed on page 10. Drain. Rinse with cold water, then drain again. To fill, place a rectangle with one point toward you. Spoon ⅓ *cup* filling diagonally across *each* rectangle just below center. Beginning at bottom *point,* roll pasta around filling. Repeat with remaining rectangles.

Cooking Pasta

Cooking Directions

3 quarts water
1 teaspoon salt
1 tablespoon olive oil
   or cooking oil
   (optional)
4 to 8 ounces pasta

● In large kettle or Dutch oven bring water and salt to boiling. I[f] desired, add olive or cooking oil to keep the pasta separated.

● Add pasta a little at a time so water continues to boil. (For long pasta, such as spaghetti, hold it at one end and dip the other end into the water. As the pasta softens, gently curl it around in the saucepan and down into the water.) Reduce heat slightly. Boil uncovered, according to the time given below or till the pasta is al dente (tender but still firm). Stir occasionally to prevent pasta from sticking. Taste the pasta often near the end of the cooking time to test for doneness.

● When pasta is done, immediately drain it in a colander. *Do not rinse.* Transfer pasta to a warm serving dish. Serve immediately. (If it is necessary to hold pasta for a short time, drain pasta and return it to the saucepan. Add 2 to 3 tablespoons *margarine* or *butter* to prevent pasta from sticking. Then cover saucepan to keep pasta warm.)

Cooking Times

Fresh Pasta	Cooking Time*
Cannelloni	2 to 3 minutes
Cappelletti	8 to 10 minutes
Fettuccine	1½ to 2 minutes
Lasagna and Mafalda	2 to 3 minutes
Linguine	1½ to 2 minutes
Manicotti	2 to 3 minutes
Noodles	1½ to 2 minutes
Ravioli	6 to 8 minutes
Tortellini	8 to 10 minutes

*If fresh pasta is dried or frozen, allow a few more minutes.

Packaged Pasta	Cooking Time
Acini di Pepe	5 to 6 minutes
Alphabets and Stellini	5 to 8 minutes
Anelli (little rings)	9 to 10 minutes
Cavatelli (curled shells)	12 minutes
Conchiglie (medium shells)	12 to 14 minutes
Conchigliette (tiny shells)	8 to 9 minutes

Packaged Pasta	Cooking Time
Conchiglioni (jumbo shells)	23 to 25 minutes
Ditalini (tiny thimbles)	10 to 12 minutes
Farfalle (bow ties)	10 minutes
Fettuccine	8 to 10 minutes
Fusilli (twisted spaghetti)	15 minutes
Lasagna and Mafalda	10 to 12 minutes
Linguine	8 to 10 minutes
Macaroni (elbow)	10 minutes
Manicotti	18 minutes
Mostaccioli	14 minutes
Noodles (medium)	6 to 8 minutes
Orzo or Rosamarina	5 to 8 minutes
Rigatoni (ridged tubes)	15 minutes
Rotelle (corkscrews)	8 to 10 minutes
Ruote (wagon wheels)	12 minutes
Spaetzle	10 to 12 minutes
Spaghetti	10 to 12 minutes
Tripolini (tiny bows)	5 to 6 minutes
Vermicelli (fine spaghetti)	5 to 7 minutes
Ziti	14 to 15 minutes

Whole Grain Pasta

Enjoy the toasty wheat flavor and whole grain texture that wheat germ adds to this pasta.

2 cups whole wheat flour
⅓ cup toasted wheat germ
½ teaspoon salt
2 beaten eggs
⅓ cup water
1 teaspoon olive oil
   or cooking oil

● In a large mixing bowl stir together *1⅔ cups* of the flour, wheat germ, and salt. Make a well in the center of the mixture.

● In a small mixing bowl combine eggs, water, and olive oil or cooking oil. Add egg mixture to flour mixture, then mix well.

● Sprinkle kneading surface with the remaining ⅓ cup flour. Turn dough out onto floured surface. Knead for 8 to 10 minutes or till smooth and elastic. Cover and let rest for 10 minutes.

● Divide dough into thirds. On a lightly floured surface roll each third into a ¹⁄₁₆-inch-thick rectangle of about 16x12 inches. *Or,* if using a pasta machine, pass dough through till ¹⁄₁₆ inch thick. Cut and shape dough as desired (see page 9). Cook or store as directed on page 10 or 14. Makes 1 pound fresh pasta.

Whole Wheat Pasta: Prepare Whole Grain Pasta as directed above, *except* use 2⅓ cups *whole wheat flour* and omit the toasted wheat germ. In a large mixing bowl stir together *2 cups* of the flour and salt. Make a well in the center of the mixture. Continue as directed above.

Pasta Diable

2⅓ cups all-purpose flour
1 tablespoon chili powder
½ teaspoon salt
2 beaten eggs
⅓ cup water
1 teaspoon olive oil
   or cooking oil

● In a large mixing bowl stir together *2 cups* of the flour, chili powder, and salt. Make a well in the center of the mixture.

● In a small mixing bowl combine eggs, water, and olive oil or cooking oil. Add egg mixture to flour mixture, then mix well.

● Sprinkle kneading surface with the remaining ⅓ cup flour. Turn dough out onto floured surface. Knead for 8 to 10 minutes or till smooth and elastic. Cover and let rest for 10 minutes.

● Divide dough into thirds. On a lightly floured surface roll each third into a ¹⁄₁₆-inch-thick rectangle of about 16x12 inches. *Or,* if using a pasta machine, pass dough through till ¹⁄₁₆ inch thick. Cut and shape dough as desired (see page 9). Cook or store as directed on page 10 or 14. Makes 1 pound fresh pasta.

Corn Pasta

1⅓ cups all-purpose flour
1 cup Masa Harina tortilla flour
½ teaspoon salt
2 beaten eggs
⅓ cup water
1 teaspoon olive oil *or* cooking oil

● In a large mixing bowl stir together *1 cup* of the all-purpos flour, tortilla flour, and salt. Make a well in center of mixture.

● In a small mixing bowl combine eggs, water, and olive o cooking oil. Add egg mixture to flour mixture, then mix well.

● Sprinkle kneading surface with remaining ⅓ cup all-purpos flour. Turn dough out onto the surface. Knead for 8 to 10 min utes or till smooth and elastic. Cover and let rest for 10 minutes

● Divide dough into thirds. On a lightly floured surface roll eac third into a 1/16-inch-thick rectangle of about 16x12 inches. O if using a pasta machine, pass dough through till 1/16 inch thick Cut and shape dough as desired (see page 9). Cook or store a directed on page 10 or 14. Makes 1 pound fresh pasta.

Carrot Pasta

Brightly colored vegetable pasta.

1 16-ounce can diced carrots, well drained
2 eggs
3¾ cups all-purpose flour
½ teaspoon salt
1 teaspoon olive oil *or* cooking oil

● In a blender container or a food processor bowl, combin carrots and eggs. Cover, then blend or process till smooth.

● In a large mixing bowl stir together *3¼ cups* of the flour an salt. Make a well in center of the mixture. Add carrot mixtur and olive or cooking oil to flour mixture, then mix well.

● Sprinkle kneading surface with the remaining ½ cup flou Turn dough out onto floured surface. Knead for 8 to 10 minute or till smooth and elastic. Cover and let rest for 10 minutes.

● Divide the dough into thirds or fourths. On a lightly floure surface roll each portion into a 1/16-inch-thick rectangle. *Or,* using a pasta machine, pass dough through till 1/16 inch thick Cut and shape dough as desired (see page 9). Cook or store a directed on page 10 or 14. Makes 1¾ pounds fresh pasta.

Beet Pasta: Prepare Carrot Pasta as above, *except* substitut one 16-ounce can sliced *beets,* well drained, for the carrots.

Tomato-Herb Pasta

Top this herby pasta with our Rich Mushroom-and-Wine Sauce (see recipe, page 17) for a wonderful side-dish combination.

3¾ cups all-purpose flour
  1 teaspoon dried basil
      or oregano, crushed
 ½ teaspoon salt
  2 beaten eggs
  1 8-ounce can tomato sauce
  1 teaspoon olive oil
      or cooking oil

● In a large mixing bowl stir together *3¼ cups* of the flour, basil or oregano, and salt. Make a well in the center of the mixture.

● In a small mixing bowl combine eggs, tomato sauce, and olive or cooking oil. Add egg mixture to flour mixture, then mix well.

● Sprinkle kneading surface with remaining ½ cup flour. Turn dough out onto the surface. Knead for 8 to 10 minutes or till dough is smooth and elastic. Cover and let rest for 10 minutes

● Divide dough into thirds or fourths. On a lightly floured surface roll each portion into a 1/16-inch-thick rectangle. *Or,* if using a pasta machine, pass dough through till 1/16 inch thick. Cut and shape dough as desired (see page 9). Cook or store as directed on page 10 or 14. Makes 1½ pounds fresh pasta.

Making Pasta in The Food Processor

You can whip up a batch of pasta dough in seconds if you have a food processor, because it will do the kneading for you.

    Place the steel blade in the food processor bowl. Add *all* the dry ingredients and eggs. Cover and process until the mixture is the consistency of cornmeal. With the processor running, slowly pour the liquid ingredients through the feed tube. Continue processing just till the dough forms a ball. Let the dough rest for 10 minutes, then continue as the recipe directs.

Parsley and Cheese Filling

1 beaten egg
1 cup ricotta *or* well-drained
    cream-style cottage
    cheese
½ cup grated Parmesan cheese
⅓ cup snipped parsley
⅛ teaspoon ground nutmeg
⅛ teaspoon grated lemon peel

● In a mixing bowl stir together the egg, ricotta or cottage cheese, Parmesan cheese, parsley, nutmeg, and lemon peel. Use the filling to stuff desired pasta, such as cappelletti, tortellini, or ravioli. Makes 1⅔ cups.

Three-Cheese Filling: Prepare Parsley and Cheese Filling as directed above, *except* stir in 1 cup shredded *mozzarella* cheese (4 ounces). Makes 2⅔ cups.

Spinach Filling

1 pound fresh spinach
    or one 10-ounce package
    frozen chopped spinach
1 tablespoon finely chopped
    onion
1 tablespoon margarine
    or butter
1 beaten egg
⅔ cup ricotta cheese
½ cup grated Parmesan cheese

● If using fresh spinach, thoroughly wash the leaves. In a large covered saucepan cook fresh spinach in a small amount of boiling salted water for 3 to 5 minutes or till tender. *Or,* if using frozen spinach, cook it according to package directions. Drain well in a colander. Remove excess moisture by squeezing spinach between several layers of paper towels. Chop spinach.

● In a saucepan cook onion in hot margarine or butter til tender but not brown. Remove from heat. Then stir in spinach, beaten egg, ricotta, and Parmesan cheese. Use to stuff desired pasta, such as tortellini, cannelloni, or manicotti. Makes 2 cups.

Storing Homemade Pasta

When you aren't going to use your pasta right after cutting or shaping it, you'll want to let it dry and then store it in the refrigerator or freezer.

● *For stuffed pasta:* Fill and shape the pasta. Lightly dust the pasta with flour and let it stand to dry for 1 hour. If you plan to use it within a day or two, put it in a covered container in the refrigerator. To keep it longer, place the pasta on a baking sheet, cover, and freeze until it is firm. Then seal the frozen pasta in moisture- and vaporproof wrap and freeze it for up to 8 months.

● *For unstuffed pasta:* Cut the pasta and spread it out on a pasta drying rack. Or, improvise your own drying rack by draping the pasta over a wire cooling rack or by hanging it over a clothes hanger. If you plan to use the pasta within a few days, let it dry overnight or until it is completely dry. Then wrap it in clear plastic wrap or foil, or place it in an airtight container. Store the pasta in the refrigerator for up to 3 days. Or, to freeze the unstuffed pasta, after drying it for 1 hour, wrap it in moisture- and vaporproof wrap and freeze it for up to 8 months.

Bolognese Sauce

Traditional Bolognese sauce calls for a combination of meats. For convenience, though, you can use 1 pound of ground beef and omit the pork or veal and the bacon.

12 ounces ground beef
 4 ounces ground pork *or* veal
 2 slices bacon, finely chopped
 1 large onion, chopped
 1 stalk celery, sliced
 ½ of a medium carrot, coarsely
      chopped
 1 28-ounce can tomatoes,
      cut up
 1 6-ounce can tomato paste
 ½ cup dry white wine
 ¼ teaspoon salt
 ⅛ teaspoon ground nutmeg
 ⅛ teaspoon pepper
12 ounces fresh pasta, cut
      into linguine, *or* 8 ounces
      spaghetti
 ⅓ cup light cream
      Grated Parmesan cheese
      (optional)

● For sauce, in a large saucepan cook beef, pork or veal, bacon, onion, celery, and carrot till meat is done and vegetables are tender. Drain off juices.

● Stir *undrained* tomatoes, tomato paste, wine, salt, nutmeg, and pepper into the meat mixture. Bring to boiling. Reduce heat. Simmer, uncovered, for 45 to 60 minutes or to desired consistency, stirring occasionally.

● Meanwhile, cook pasta as directed on page 10. Drain pasta in a colander, then transfer to a warm serving dish.

● Stir cream into the sauce. Then spoon sauce over pasta. If desired, pass Parmesan cheese. Makes 5 main-dish servings.

Fresh Tomato-Herb Sauce

Some fresh tomatoes have more water in them than others. So the time it takes to simmer the sauce down to 1½ cups may vary.

 1 medium onion, chopped
 1 tablespoon margarine
      or butter
 2 pounds fresh tomatoes,
      cut up (6 medium)
 2 teaspoons snipped fresh
      marjoram *or* ¾ teaspoon
      dried marjoram, crushed
 2 teaspoons snipped fresh
      basil *or* ¾ teaspoon dried
      basil, crushed
 ½ teaspoon sugar
 ½ teaspoon salt
 8 ounces fresh pasta, cut into
      linguine *or* fettuccine, *or*
      1⅔ cups corkscrew
      macaroni (rotelle)

● For sauce, in a large saucepan cook onion in hot margarine or butter till tender but not brown. Stir in tomatoes, marjoram, basil, sugar, and salt. Bring to boiling. Reduce heat. Simmer, uncovered, for 30 mintues, stirring occasionally.

● Pass sauce through a food mill or a sieve. Discard skins, seeds, and any other solids. Return sauce to the saucepan. Bring to boiling. Reduce heat. Simmer, uncovered, for 10 to 15 minutes more or till the sauce is reduced to *1½ cups,* stirring occasionally.

● Meanwhile, cook pasta as directed on page 10. Drain pasta in a colander, then transfer to a warm serving dish. Spoon sauce over pasta. Makes 6 side-dish servings.

Ratatouille-Topped Pas

Ratatouille-Topped Pasta

½ cup chopped onion
2 cloves garlic, minced
1 tablespoon cooking oil
1 16-ounce can whole
 tomatoes, drained and
 cut up, *or* 4 medium
 tomatoes, peeled and
 chopped
1½ cups cubed peeled eggplant
1 cup sliced zucchini
1 8-ounce can tomato sauce
½ cup chopped green pepper
2 tablespoons snipped parsley
½ teaspoon dried oregano,
 crushed
½ teaspoon dried basil,
 crushed
¼ teaspoon sugar
¼ teaspoon salt
⅛ teaspoon pepper
4 teaspoons cornstarch
6 ounces fresh spinach *or*
 plain pasta, cut into
 fettuccine, *or* 4 ounces
 packaged fettuccine
 Grated Parmesan cheese

● For sauce, in a large saucepan cook onion and garlic in hot oil till tender but not brown. Stir in tomatoes, eggplant, zucchini, tomato sauce, green pepper, parsley, oregano, basil, sugar, salt and pepper. Bring to boiling. Reduce heat. Cover and simmer mixture for 15 to 20 minutes or to desired consistency, stirring occasionally.

● Stir together cornstarch and 1 tablespoon *water*. Stir into tomato mixture. Cook and stir mixture till thickened and bubbly. Then cook and stir for 2 minutes more.

● Cook pasta as directed on page 10. Drain pasta in a colander, then transfer to a warm serving dish. Spoon sauce over pasta. Sprinkle with *1 tablespoon* Parmesan cheese. If desired, pass additional Parmesan cheese. Makes 6 side-dish servings.

Rich Mushroom-and-Wine Sauce

Simmering the sauce will deliciously concentrate the mellow wine flavor in the mushrooms.

2 cups fresh mushrooms,
 sliced
7 medium green onions, sliced
2 tablespoons margarine
 or butter
½ cup dry white wine
1½ teaspoons snipped fresh
 basil *or* ½ teaspoon dried
 basil, crushed
¼ teaspoon salt
⅔ cup whipping cream
6 ounces fresh pasta, cut
 into linguine, *or* 4 ounces
 packaged egg *or* whole
 wheat linguine

● For sauce, in a medium saucepan cook the mushrooms and onions in hot margarine or butter till tender. Stir in wine, basil, and salt. Bring to boiling. Reduce heat. Simmer, uncovered, about 15 minutes or till the liquid is reduced to *2 to 4 tablespoons*, stirring occasionally. Stir in cream. Then cook and stir about 5 minutes more or till mixture thickens.

● Meanwhile, cook pasta as directed on page 10. Drain pasta in a colander, then transfer to a warm serving dish. Spoon sauce over pasta. Makes 6 side-dish servings.

Old-Fashioned Spaghetti with Meatballs

1 cup fresh mushrooms,
    sliced
1 small green pepper,
    chopped
1 small onion, chopped
1 clove garlic, minced
2 tablespoons margarine
    or butter
1 16-ounce can tomatoes,
    cut up
1 15-ounce can tomato sauce
1 teaspoon sugar
1 teaspoon dried basil,
    crushed
½ teaspoon dried marjoram,
    crushed
½ teaspoon dried oregano,
    crushed
1 beaten egg
½ cup soft bread crumbs
2 tablespoons snipped parsley
¼ teaspoon ground thyme
1 pound ground beef
1 tablespoon cooking oil
8 ounces spaghetti *or*
    12 ounces fresh pasta, cut
    into linguine

● For sauce, in a Dutch oven cook mushrooms, green pepper, onion, and garlic in hot margarine or butter till tender. Stir in *undrained* tomatoes, tomato sauce, sugar, basil, marjoram, oregano, and ¼ teaspoon *salt*. Bring to boiling. Reduce heat. Simmer, uncovered, for 35 to 40 minutes or to desired consistency, stirring occasionally.

● Meanwhile, for meatballs, in a medium mixing bowl combine egg, bread crumbs, parsley, thyme, ¼ teaspoon *salt,* and ⅛ teaspoon *pepper.* Add beef, then mix well. Shape mixture into 1½-inch meatballs. In a large skillet cook meatballs in hot oil till brown. Using a slotted spoon, transfer meatballs to the sauce mixture. Then simmer, uncovered, for 10 to 15 minutes more or till meatballs are cooked.

● Cook pasta as directed on page 10. Drain pasta in a colander, then transfer to a warm serving dish. Spoon sauce and meatballs over pasta. Makes 5 servings.

Carbonara-Style Linguine

The heat from the hot pasta cooks the eggs and cream into a delicious coating.

3 slightly beaten eggs
12 ounces fresh pasta, cut
    into linguine, *or* 8 ounces
    packaged linguine *or*
    vermicelli
4 ounces fully cooked
    boneless ham, cut into
    thin strips
¼ cup snipped parsley
2 tablespoons light cream
    or milk
⅛ teaspoon white pepper
    Dash ground nutmeg
⅔ cup grated Parmesan cheese

● Remove eggs from the refrigerator and let eggs stand till they reach room temperature.

● Cook pasta as directed on page 10, *except* add the ham strips the last 1 minute of cooking. Meanwhile, in a medium mixing bowl stir together eggs, parsley, cream or milk, pepper, and nutmeg.

● When pasta is al dente, drain pasta and ham in a colander. Then immediately return them to the hot saucepan. Add egg mixture. Toss till coated. Then add Parmesan cheese and toss again. Serve immediately. Makes 4 servings.

Carbonara-Style Linguine

Classic Lasagna

4 ounces bulk pork sausage
1 cup sliced fresh mushrooms
⅓ cup chopped onion
1 clove garlic, minced
1 16-ounce can tomatoes, cut up
1 15-ounce can tomato sauce
1 teaspoon sugar
1 teaspoon dried basil, crushed
1 teaspoon dried oregano, crushed
½ teaspoon celery salt
1 beaten egg
1 cup ricotta *or* cream-style cottage cheese, drained
½ cup grated Parmesan cheese
5 ounces fresh pasta, cut into lasagna noodles, *or* 6 packaged lasagna noodles
1 cup shredded mozzarella cheese (4 ounces)

● For sauce, in a saucepan cook sausage, mushrooms, onion, and garlic till sausage is browned and onion is tender. Drain off juices. Stir in *undrained* tomatoes, tomato sauce, sugar, basil, oregano, celery salt, and ⅛ teaspoon *pepper.* Bring to boiling. Reduce heat. Simmer, uncovered, for 35 to 40 minutes or to desired consistency. Meanwhile, in a bowl stir together egg, ricotta or cottage cheese, and ¼ *cup* of the Parmesan cheese; set aside.

● Cook pasta as directed on page 10, *except* cook till *almost al* dente (allow 1 to 1½ minutes for fresh pasta; 8 to 9 minutes for packaged pasta). Drain pasta in a colander. Rinse with cold water, then drain again.

● To assemble, arrange *3* noodles in a greased 10x6x2-inch baking dish, trimming noodles to fit. Top with *half* of the ricotta cheese mixture. Then top with *half* of the sauce. Sprinkle with *half* of the mozzarella cheese. Repeat layers of noodles, cheese mixture, and sauce; reserve remaining mozzarella cheese. Sprinkle with remaining Parmesan cheese. Cover with foil. Bake in a 350° oven for 35 minutes. Uncover and sprinkle with remaining mozzarella cheese. Bake for 5 to 10 minutes more or till heated. Let stand for 10 minutes before serving. Serves 6.

Saucy Italian Manicotti

1 pound bulk Italian sausage
1 cup chopped carrot
½ cup chopped onion
1 clove garlic, minced
1 28-ounce can tomatoes
1 6-ounce can tomato paste
2 teaspoons Italian seasoning
5 ounces fresh pasta, cut into manicotti rectangles, *or* 8 packaged manicotti shells
¾ cup shredded mozzarella cheese

● For filling, in a large skillet cook sausage, carrot, onion, and garlic till sausage is browned and vegetables are tender. Drain.

● Drain tomatoes, reserving *1 cup* juice. Set juice aside. Chop tomatoes. Stir tomatoes, tomato paste, and Italian seasoning into sausage mixture. Bring to boiling. Reduce heat to medium-low. Cook, uncovered, for 10 minutes, stirring occasionally.

● Meanwhile, cook pasta as directed on page 10; drain. Rinse with cold water, then drain again. To fill, for fresh manicotti spoon ⅓ cup filling diagonally across *each* rectangle, then roll pasta around filling. For packaged manicotti, spoon about ¼ cup of the filling into *each* shell. Set remaining filling aside.

● Arrange filled manicotti in a 12x7½x2-inch baking dish. Stir reserved tomato juice into remaining filling. Pour over manicotti. Cover with foil. Bake in a 350° oven for 30 to 35 minutes or till heated through. Uncover and sprinkle with cheese. Bake for 2 to 3 minutes more or till cheese is melted. Makes 4 servings.

Linguine with White Clam Sauce

2 6½- *or* 7½-ounce cans
   minced clams
6 ounces fresh pasta, cut into
   linguine, *or* 4 ounces
   packaged linguine
¼ cup thinly sliced green
   onion
1 clove garlic, minced
2 tablespoons margarine
   or butter
2 tablespoons all-purpose
   flour
⅛ teaspoon pepper
¾ cup milk
1 cup frozen broccoli cuts,
   thawed, *or* 2 tablespoons
   sliced pitted ripe olives
2 tablespoons snipped parsley
2 tablespoons dry white wine
   Grated Parmesan cheese

● Drain clams, reserving ¼ *cup* juice. Set clams and juice aside. Cook pasta as directed on page 10. Drain pasta in a colander, then transfer to a serving dish and cover to keep warm.

● Meanwhile, for sauce, in a medium saucepan cook green onion and garlic in hot margarine or butter till onion is tender but not brown. Stir in flour and pepper. Add milk. Cook and stir till thickened and bubbly, then cook and stir for 1 minute more. Add clams, reserved juice, broccoli (if using), parsley, and wine. Cook and stir till mixture is heated through.

● To serve, pour sauce over hot linguine. If using olives, add them to pasta-sauce mixture. Gently toss till coated. Sprinkle with Parmesan cheese. Serve immediately. Makes 2 servings.

How to eat pasta

Is there a proper way to eat pasta? One school of thought says you should catch a few strands of pasta on a fork. Then, with the tines rested against a spoon, twist the fork to wrap up the pasta. Yet, others say you should spear a few strands on a fork. Then with the tip of the fork rested against the plate (*not* a spoon), twirl the fork and the pasta.

Our advice? Use whatever works for you.

Fettuccine Alfredo

The cheese, cream, and butter thicken and form a rich sauce when tossed with the hot pasta.

⅓ cup light cream *or* whipping
    cream
3 tablespoons margarine
    or butter, cut up
8 ounces packaged fettuccine
½ cup grated Parmesan cheese
    Fresh coarsely cracked
    black pepper

● Remove cream and margarine or butter from the refrigerator and let stand till they reach room temperature.

● Cook pasta as directed on page 10.

● When pasta is al dente, drain it in a colander. Then immediately return pasta to the hot saucepan. Add the Parmesan cheese, light cream or whipping cream, and margarine or butter. Toss till pasta is well coated. Transfer to a warm serving dish. Sprinkle with pepper. Serve immediately. Serves 4.

Chicken Couscous

This North African favorite gets its name from the grain.

1 2½- to 3-pound broiler-fryer
    chicken, cut up and
    skinned
1 tablespoon cooking oil
2 medium onions, coarsely
    chopped
1 clove garlic, minced
1 15-ounce can garbanzo
    beans, drained and rinsed
1 10½-ounce can tomato
    puree
1 7½-ounce can tomatoes,
    cut up
½ cup raisins
½ cup water
2 bay leaves
6 inches stick cinnamon
1½ teaspoons chili powder
½ teaspoon ground ginger
½ teaspoon ground cumin
4 cups desired fresh
    vegetables*
1 cup quick-cooking couscous

● In a Dutch oven brown chicken pieces on one side in hot oil for 7 minutes. Turn chicken pieces over, then add onion and garlic. Cook about 8 minutes more or till chicken is browned and onion is tender.

● Stir in garbanzo beans, tomato puree, *undrained* tomatoes, raisins, water, bay leaves, cinnamon, chili powder, ginger, and cumin. Then stir in vegetables. Bring to boiling. Reduce heat. Cover and simmer about 30 minutes or till chicken and vegetables are tender. Discard bay leaves and cinnamon sticks.

● Meanwhile, stir couscous into 1 cup *boiling water.* Remove from the heat. Let stand, covered, for 3 to 4 minutes or just till liquid is absorbed. To serve, mound couscous and chicken mixture on a serving platter. Makes 6 servings.

*For vegetables, choose any of the following: carrots, cut into ¼-inch slices; celery, cut into 1-inch pieces; zucchini, halved lengthwise and cut into ½-inch slices; green pepper, cut into bite-size pieces; turnip, peeled and cut into ¼-inch cubes; and chopped cabbage.

Chicken Couscous

Sausage-Spaetzle Soup

The Germans created the pasta spaetzle (SHPETS-luh) by pressing batter through a colander into boiling liquid.

8 ounces bulk pork sausage
1 stalk celery, sliced
½ of a medium onion, chopped
1 clove garlic, minced
3 cups water
1 7½-ounce can tomatoes, cut up
½ of a 10-ounce package spaetzle
1 carrot, sliced
1 tablespoon instant beef bouillon granules
2 bay leaves

● In a large saucepan cook pork sausage, celery, onion, and garlic till the sausage is browned and vegetables are nearly tender. Drain off juices.

● Stir water, *undrained* tomatoes, spaetzle, carrot, and bouillon granules into meat mixture. Add bay leaves. Bring to boiling. Reduce heat. Cover and simmer for 15 to 20 minutes or till spaetzle is done. Remove bay leaves. Skim off fat. Serves 4.

Microwave Beef 'n' Noodle Casserole

Our home economists tested this recipe in countertop microwave ovens that provided 600 to 700 watts of cooking power. The cooking times are approximate because microwave ovens vary by manufacture.

2 ounces (1½ cups) packaged medium green *or* plain noodles
1 pound ground beef *or* pork
½ cup chopped onion
1 8-ounce can whole kernel corn, drained
1 7½-ounce can semi-condensed cream of mushroom soup
½ of an 8-ounce container soft-style cream cheese
½ teaspoon dried savory, crushed
½ teaspoon dried marjoram, crushed
2 teaspoons margarine *or* butter
¼ cup soft bread crumbs
2 tablespoons grated Parmesan cheese

● Cook pasta on the range-top as directed on page 10. Drain pasta in a colander.

● Meanwhile, crumble ground meat into a 2-quart microwave-safe casserole. Add onion. Micro-cook, covered, on 100% power (high) for 5 to 7 minutes or till meat is no longer pink and onion is tender, stirring after every 3 minutes. Drain off juices.

● Stir cooked noodles, corn, soup, cream cheese, savory, marjoram, and ⅛ teaspoon *pepper* into casserole. Cook, covered, on high for 5 to 7 minutes or till heated through, stirring after every 3 minutes. Set casserole aside.

● Place margarine or butter in a small microwave-safe mixing bowl. Cook, uncovered, on high for 30 to 45 seconds or till melted. Stir in bread crumbs and Parmesan cheese. Then sprinkle over meat-noodle mixture. Makes 6 servings.

Florentine Lasagna Rosettes

Dining alone? Here's an elegant entrée just for one.

½ of a 10-ounce package
    frozen chopped spinach,
    thawed and drained
    (½ cup)
1 packaged lasagna noodle
    (1 ounce)
1 single-serving envelope
    instant cream of chicken
    soup mix
½ cup hot water
¼ cup shredded Swiss
    or Colby cheese
4 ounces ground raw turkey,
    beef, *or* pork
1 tablespoon chopped onion
¼ teaspoon dried thyme,
    crushed

● Squeeze excess liquid from spinach, then set aside. Cook the lasagna noodle as directed on page 10. Drain in a colander.

● For sauce, in a small saucepan combine soup mix, hot water, and cheese. Cook and stir over medium heat till the cheese is melted. Remove from heat and set aside.

● In a medium skillet cook the ground turkey, beef, or pork and onion till meat is no longer pink and onion is tender. Drain off juices. Stir spinach, thyme, and *half* of the cheese sauce into the meat mixture.

● To assemble, cut lasagna noodle lengthwise in half. In an individual greased baking dish curl each noodle half into a rosette about 2½ inches in diameter. Spoon meat mixture into the lasagna rosettes. Then spoon remaining cheese sauce over rosettes. Cover with foil. Bake in a 350° oven for 25 to 30 minutes or till heated through. To serve, spoon extra sauce from dish over rosettes. Makes 1 serving.

Shaping and filling the Florentine Lasagna Rosettes
Cook and cool a lasagna noodle. Then cut the noodle lengthwise in half.

In the baking dish, place the noodle pieces, cut sides down, and wrap them around in a spiral fashion to make a 2½-inch rosette shape. To fill, just spoon the meat mixture into the rosettes.

Lasagna Pie

9 *or* 10 packaged lasagna noodles
1½ cups ricotta cheese
3 tablespoons milk
½ teaspoon dried basil, crushed
¼ teaspoon pepper
1 pound ground raw turkey
1½ cups coarsely shredded carrot
½ cup chopped onion
1 clove garlic, minced
1 15-ounce can tomato sauce
½ teaspoon dried oregano, crushed
¼ teaspoon salt
2 small tomatoes, thinly sliced
  Snipped fresh basil (optional)

● Cook pasta as directed on page 10, then drain. Set noodles aside. Meanwhile, in a small mixing bowl stir together ricotta cheese, milk, dried basil, and pepper. Set cheese mixture aside.

● For filling, in a large skillet cook turkey, carrot, onion, and garlic till turkey is no longer pink and carrot is tender. Drain off juices. Stir in tomato sauce, oregano, and salt. Cook till heated.

● To assemble, line a lightly greased 9-inch springform pan with noodles, extending noodles over sides of pan. Layer *half o*f the turkey mixture, *1 cup* of the ricotta mixture, then remaining turkey mixture. Trim noodles so that 3 inches extend over sides of pan. Discard trimmings. Fold noodle ends over turkey mixture. Cover with foil.

● Place the springform pan on a 15x10x1-inch baking pan. Bake in a 375° oven for 30 minutes. Spread remaining ricotta mixture over top. Place tomatoes around edges, overlapping slightly. Cover and bake for 20 minutes more or till heated through. Let stand 10 minutes before serving. If desired, garnish with fresh basil. Cut into wedges to serve. Serves 6.

Arranging the noodles
When you're ready to assemble the Lasagna Pie, place the end of the first noodle in the center of a lightly greased 9-inch springform pan, then extend the noodle over the side of the pan. Place the remaining noodles in the pan, spoke fashion. One end of each noodle should extend over the edge of the pan. The other ends of the noodles should overlap just slightly in the center of the pan so the filling won't leak out.

Pasta with Scallops and Wine Sauce

If you like, use spinach pasta for a splash of color.

12 ounces fresh *or* frozen
    scallops
2 ounces packaged spaghetti,
    fettuccine, *or* linguine
¼ cup chopped onion
1 clove garlic, minced
1 tablespoon margarine
    or butter
½ cup dry white wine
1 teaspoon dried basil,
    crushed
¼ teaspoon salt
¼ teaspoon dried oregano,
    crushed
1 tablespoon cold water
2 teaspoons cornstarch
2 medium tomatoes, seeded
    and chopped (about 1 cup)
¼ cup grated Parmesan cheese
2 tablespoons snipped parsley

● Thaw scallops, if frozen. Cook pasta as directed on page 10. Drain pasta in a colander, then transfer to a serving dish and cover to keep warm.

● Cut any large scallops in half. For sauce, in a saucepan cook onion and garlic in hot margarine or butter till tender but not brown. Stir in wine, basil, salt, and oregano. Bring to boiling, then add scallops. Return to boiling.

● Meanwhile, stir together water and cornstarch. Stir cornstarch mixture into boiling scallop mixture. Cook and stir till thickened and bubbly. Cook and stir for 2 minutes more or till scallops are opaque. Stir in chopped tomatoes.

● To serve, pour sauce over hot pasta. Add Parmesan cheese and parsley. Gently toss till coated. Makes 4 servings.

Macaroni Cloud in a Mug

You'll be floating on cloud nine when you spoon into this heavenly macaroni and cheese.

½ cup whole wheat *or* plain
    elbow macaroni
2 tablespoons finely chopped
    green pepper
1 tablespoon finely chopped
    onion
1 cup milk
4 teaspoons cornstarch
¼ teaspoon salt
    Dash pepper
    Dash bottled hot pepper
    sauce
1½ cups shredded cheddar
    cheese (6 ounces)
1 cup frozen whole kernel
    corn, thawed
2 egg yolks
2 egg whites
⅛ teaspoon cream of tartar

● Cook pasta as directed on page 10, *except* cook macaroni for 6 minutes. Add green pepper and onion, and cook for 2 minutes more. Drain. Rinse with cold water, then drain again.

● For cheese mixture, in the saucepan stir together milk and cornstarch. Stir in salt, pepper, and hot pepper sauce. Cook and stir till thickened and bubbly. Reduce heat to low. Add cheese and corn. Cook and stir just till melted. Remove from heat.

● In a medium mixing bowl lightly beat egg yolks with a wire whisk or fork. Slowly add cheese mixture, stirring constantly. Fold in macaroni mixture, then cool slightly. In a small mixing bowl beat egg whites and cream of tartar till stiff peaks form (tips stand straight). Fold egg whites into macaroni mixture.

● Spoon macaroni mixture into four 12-ounce ovenproof mugs or 10-ounce custard cups, leaving a ¼-inch headspace in each. Place on a baking sheet or shallow baking pan. Bake in a 325° oven for 30 to 35 minutes or till the tops are golden brown and a knife inserted near the centers comes out clean. Serves 4.

Beef and Pasta Salad

If you prefer peeled tomatoes in your salad, just dip the tomatoes into the boiling water before you cook the pasta. The skins will slip right off.

1½ cups corkscrew macaroni
    (rotelle)
1 10-ounce package frozen
    cut broccoli
6 ounces thinly sliced
    cooked beef
1 6-ounce jar marinated
    artichoke hearts, drained
2 small tomatoes
1 cup crumbled feta cheese
    (4 ounces)
½ cup Caesar salad dressing

● Cook pasta as directed on page 10, *except* add broccoli after 6 minutes. Return to boiling. Reduce heat slightly and continue boiling, uncovered, for 2 to 3 minutes more or till broccoli is nearly tender. Drain in a colander. Rinse with cold water, then drain again.

● Meanwhile, cut the beef into julienne strips. Cut up any large artichoke hearts. Cut tomatoes into small wedges.

● For salad, in a large salad bowl combine beef, artichoke hearts, tomatoes, feta cheese, and pasta mixture. Pour dressing over mixture. Then gently toss till coated. If desired, place in the freezer for 10 to 15 minutes to chill before serving. Serves 4.

Pasta Salad Niçoise

This Mediterranean salad traditionally uses marinated cooked potatoes; our version uses marinated pasta shells for a new taste.

⅓ cup medium pasta shells
    (conchiglie) *or*
    corkscrew macaroni
    (rotelle)
¼ teaspoon dried dillweed
¼ cup oil-and-vinegar salad
    dressing
1 3¼-ounce can tuna
⅓ cup fresh *or* frozen green
    beans
    Lettuce leaves
    Radicchio leaves (optional)
4 pitted ripe olives (optional)
3 *or* 4 tomato slices
1 hard-cooked egg, quartered
    (optional)
    Thinly sliced green onion
    (optional)
    Anchovy fillet (optional)
    Garlic toast (optional)

● Cook pasta as directed on page 10. Drain in a colander. Rinse with cold water, then drain again. Transfer pasta to a small mixing bowl.

● Stir dillweed into salad dressing. Add *2 tablespoons* of the dressing mixture to the pasta in the bowl. Gently toss till coated. Cover and chill for several hours or overnight. Drain tuna, then transfer to another small mixing bowl. Add *1 tablespoon* of the dressing mixture and toss till mixed. Cover and chill. Cook green beans till nearly tender, then cover and chill.

● To serve, arrange lettuce leaves and radicchio leaves (if desired) on a salad plate. Then arrange pasta, tuna, beans, olives, tomato slices, and egg on top of the lettuce. If desired, top with green onion and anchovy fillet. Drizzle with remaining salad dressing. If desired, serve with garlic toast. Makes 1 serving.

Pasta Salad Niçoise

Sweet-and-Sour Pasta Salad

To keep the broccoli bright green and the nuts crunchy, add them just before serving.

1 tablespoon cornstarch
1 tablespoon brown sugar
½ teaspoon ground ginger
¼ teaspoon garlic powder
1 6-ounce can unsweetened
   pineapple juice
¼ cup white wine vinegar
2 tablespoons water
2 tablespoons soy sauce
1½ cups broccoli flowerets
2 cups tiny pasta bows
   (tripolini)
1 8-ounce package frozen
   cooked shrimp, thawed
1 medium carrot, thinly bias
   sliced
½ cup peanuts *or* cashews

● For dressing, in a small saucepan combine cornstarch, brown sugar, ginger, and garlic powder. Stir in juice, vinegar, water, and soy sauce. Cook and stir till thickened and bubbly. Cook and stir for 2 minutes more. Remove from heat and cool.

● Meanwhile, in a medium covered saucepan cook broccoli in a small amount of lightly salted boiling water for 4 to 5 minutes or till nearly tender, then drain. Rinse with cold water, then drain again. Cover and chill.

● In another saucepan cook pasta as directed on page 10. Drain in a colander. Rinse with cold water, then drain again.

● In a medium salad bowl combine pasta, shrimp, and carrot. Pour dressing over pasta mixture. Gently toss till coated. Cover and chill for 2 to 8 hours, gently tossing mixture occasionally.

● To serve, add chilled broccoli and peanuts or cashews. Gently toss till mixed. Makes 4 servings.

Tuna and Pasta Salad

Our Test Kitchen suggests serving this colorful salad on lettuce-lined plates.

2 cups tiny pasta shells
   (conchigliette)
1 12½-ounce can tuna,
   drained and flaked
½ cup shredded Swiss cheese
½ cup shredded cheddar
   cheese
1 stalk celery, sliced
¼ cup sliced green onion
½ cup mayonnaise *or* salad
   dressing
½ cup plain yogurt
1 tablespoon milk
½ teaspoon garlic salt
½ teaspoon dried dillweed
   Milk
1 medium tomato, seeded and
   cut into thin strips
   Bibb lettuce *or* Boston
   lettuce leaves
   Lemon *or* lime wedges

● Cook pasta as directed on page 10. Drain pasta in a colander. Rinse with cold water, then drain again.

● In a medium mixing bowl combine pasta, tuna, Swiss cheese, cheddar cheese, celery, and green onion.

● For dressing, in a small mixing bowl combine the mayonnaise or salad dressing, yogurt, 1 tablespoon milk, garlic salt, and dillweed. Stir till well blended. Pour dressing over pasta mixture. Gently toss till coated. Cover and chill for 2 to 8 hours.

● To serve, if necessary, stir in a few tablespoons of additional milk to moisten mixture. Add tomato and gently toss. Line 6 salad plates with lettuce. Spoon pasta mixture onto the plates. Garnish with lemon or lime wedges. Makes 6 servings.

Tortellini and Spinach Salad

Combine salmon, spinach, and tortellini for a delicious, colorful salad.

1 7-ounce package cheese-
   filled tortellini
⅓ cup salad oil
¼ cup lemon juice
1 tablespoon Dijon-style
   mustard
½ teaspoon salt
¼ teaspoon pepper
1 clove garlic, minced
6 cups torn spinach
15 ounces cooked salmon* *or*
   one 15½-ounce can red
   salmon, drained, skin and
   bones removed, broken
   into chunks, and chilled
1 cup pitted ripe olives,
   drained and cut in half
2 green onions, thinly sliced

● Cook tortellini according to package directions. Drain pasta in a colander, then transfer to a large salad bowl.

● Meanwhile, for dressing, in a screw-top jar combine salad oil, lemon juice, mustard, salt, pepper, and garlic. Cover and shake well. Pour dressing over warm tortellini. Gently toss till coated. Cover and chill about 2 hours, tossing the mixture occasionally.

● For salad, add spinach, salmon, olives, and green onions to tortellini-dressing mixture. Gently toss till coated. Serves 6.

*For 15 ounces of cooked salmon, start with 3 fresh *or* frozen *salmon steaks,* cut ¾ to 1 inch thick (about 1½ pounds total). Thaw salmon, if frozen. In a medium skillet combine 1 cup *water,* 1 tablespoon thinly sliced *green onion,* 1 *bay leaf,* ¼ teaspoon *salt,* and dash *pepper.* Bring to boiling; add salmon. Reduce heat. Cover and simmer for 5 to 10 minutes or till salmon flakes easily with a fork. Drain and cool salmon slightly. Then remove skin and bones. Break the salmon steaks into large chunks. Cover and chill before using in the salad.

Salad Greens Can Make A Salad

A serving of delicious salad on a pretty plate can be made elegant with some of the lovely salad greens on the market, such as escarole, curly endive, Oriental kale, mustard greens, or even crinkly leaf lettuce. To prepare salad greens, wash them in lots of cold water. Then place the greens on paper towels or a clean kitchen towel and gently pat dry.

Reclosable plastic bags are great for storing salad greens in your refrigerator till you are ready to use them. When properly stored, greens may be kept for three or four days.

Vacuum-packed Tortellini

No-Boil Lasagna

Egg Capellini

Spinach Fettuccine

Tomato and Egg Ravioli

Lasagna Sheets

Quick-Cooking

Pastas

Some pasta products are made for convenience. These items cook fast and are easy to store. The availability of specialty pastas varies by region and supermarket.

If you don't find the products at your store, ask the manager to look into stocking them for you.

SHELF-STABLE TORTELLINI: Even though it's filled with meat or cheese, you can store this tortellini right on the shelf, saving valuable refrigerator or freezer space. Both dried and vacuum-packed tortellini are available, but the latter cooks about twice as fast.

NO-BOIL LASAGNA: That's right—no boiling before layering this noodle. For De Rosa's lasagna shown here, simply wet it, layer with cheese and sauce, then bake or micro-cook.

Another lasagna sheet is precooked, then frozen. Use it from the package as you would a cooked lasagna noodle. Look for this convenience product in the freezer case next to the fresh-frozen pasta.

FRESH AND FRESH-FROZEN PASTA: These pastas cook four to five times faster than dried pasta. Spinach fettuccine, egg capellini, tomato and egg ravioli, and lasagna sheets (shown here) are just a start. Check out the variety at your market. The smaller and thinner the pasta, the quicker it cooks.

Sauces

When you're in a pinch at mealtime, whip up a fast home-cooked pasta dish. Toss one of these simple sauces with *4 ounces* of your favorite pasta that's been cooked and drained. Serve as a fast and fancy companion to broiled poultry, fish, beef, or pork. Better yet, toss some cut-up cooked meat in with the pasta for a lickety-split main dish.

● Cook 1 teaspoon *bottled minced garlic* in a little *olive* or *cooking oil* till tender. Stir in ¼ teaspoon crushed *dried tarragon* and a little *salt* and *pepper*. Toss with 2 cups hot cooked *vegetables* and desired *pasta*.

● In the warm saucepan used to cook the desired *pasta*, pour ¼ cup *light cream*, ¼ cup grated *Parmesan cheese*, and 1 tablespoon *margarine* or *butter* over pasta. Toss gently till well coated. Sprinkle with cracked *pepper* and snipped *parsley*.

● Heat ½ of an 8-ounce container *soft-style cream cheese with chives and onion*, 3 tablespoons *milk*, 1 tablespoon *margarine* or *butter*, and teaspoon *dried parsley flakes* over medium-low heat till cheese melts and mixture is warm, stirring occasionally. Stir in ¼ cup grated *Romano cheese*. Toss with desired *pasta*.

● In the warm saucepan used to cook the desired *pasta*, toss ½ cup shredded *Monterey Jack cheese with jalapeño peppers* or *caraway*; one 2-ounce jar *diced pimiento*, drained; ⅓ cup *whipping cream*; and a little *salt* with the pasta. Cook and stir over medium heat for 3 to 4 minutes or till the cheese melts and sauce thickens.

● Toss ¼ cup *sour cream dip* (any flavor) with the desired *pasta*. Sprinkle with grated *Parmesan cheese*.

Chinese Noodle Skillet

6 ounces vermicelli (fine spaghetti) *or* fusilli (twisted spaghetti)
1 16-ounce package frozen mixed broccoli, baby carrots, and water chestnuts
3 tablespoons water
3 tablespoons dry sherry
2 tablespoons soy sauce
2 teaspoons cornstarch
¼ teaspoon ground ginger
¼ teaspoon garlic powder
1 tablespoon cooking oil
8 ounces fully cooked boneless ham, cut into julienne strips

● Cook pasta as directed on page 10. Drain in a colander. Then return pasta to the saucepan. Add a little *margarine* or *butter*. Toss till coated. Cover and set aside.

● Meanwhile, place vegetables in the colander. Run *hot water* over vegetables just till thawed. Drain vegetables well; set aside. For sauce, in a custard cup stir together water, sherry, soy sauce, cornstarch, ginger, and garlic powder. Set sauce aside.

● Preheat a wok or large skillet over high heat. Add oil. (Add more oil as needed during cooking.) Cook and stir vegetables for 1 to 2 minutes or till nearly tender. Add ham. Cook and stir for 1 minute. Then push vegetables and ham from center of wok.

● Stir sauce mixture. Add mixture to center of wok or skillet. Cook and stir till bubbly. Then cook and stir for 2 minutes more. Gently stir in vegetables and ham just till coated.

● To serve, transfer pasta to a warm serving dish. Spoon vegetable-ham mixture over pasta. Makes 4 servings.

Hearty Noodle Stew

Oregano and marjoram give this stew a delicious Italian twist.

1 14½-ounce can tomatoes, cut up
1¾ cups water
1 9-ounce package frozen Italian green beans
½ cup chopped onion
1 3-ounce package Oriental noodles with chicken flavor
1 teaspoon dried oregano, crushed
1 teaspoon dried marjoram, crushed
1 16-ounce fully cooked smoked turkey sausage link
Grated Parmesan cheese (optional)

● In a large saucepan combine *undrained* tomatoes, water, beans, onion, seasoning packet from the Oriental noodles, oregano, and marjoram. Bring to boiling.

● Meanwhile, cut sausage link lengthwise in half. Then cut halves into 1-inch pieces. Slightly break up Oriental noodles.

● Add Oriental noodles to the tomato mixture in saucepan. Then add sausage. Return mixture to boiling. Reduce heat. Cover and simmer for 3 to 5 minutes or till noodles are tender.

● To serve, ladle stew into individual bowls. If desired, sprinkle with Parmesan cheese. Makes 4 servings.

Rush-Hour Simmer Dinner

The Italians call fine spaghetti "vermicelli." You can buy it in straight rods or as clusters, called nested vermicelli.

2 6¾-ounce cans chunk-style chicken
1 8-ounce can whole small carrots, drained
4 bundles nested vermicelli (fine spaghetti)
1 cup frozen peas
1 small onion, thinly sliced
1½ cups chicken broth
1 teaspoon dried tarragon, crushed

● In a large skillet arrange *undrained* chicken, carrots, pasta, peas, and onion slices. Add chicken broth and tarragon.

● Bring to boiling. Reduce heat. Cover and simmer for 15 to 20 minutes or till pasta is al dente (tender but still firm), stirring occasionally. Serve at once. Makes 4 servings.

Spicy Italian Casserole

Put away your casserole dish and grab your skillet. Dinner will be on the table in a hurry when you make this casserole-like dish on top of the range instead of in the oven.

1½ cups elbow macaroni
1 pound ground turkey sausage
1 15½-ounce jar meatless spaghetti sauce with tomato, garlic, and onion
¼ teaspoon crushed red pepper
1 4-ounce package shredded mozzarella cheese (1 cup)

● Cook pasta as directed on page 10. Drain well in a colander.

● Meanwhile, in a large skillet cook turkey sausage till no longer pink. Drain off juices.

● Stir cooked macaroni, spaghetti sauce, crushed red pepper, and ¼ cup *water* into the sausage in the skillet. Then cover and cook over medium-high heat about 3 minutes or till heated, stirring occasionally.

● Sprinkle with cheese. Cover and cook about 1 minute or till cheese is just melted. Makes 6 servings.

Rush-Hour Simmer Dinner

Oriental Chicken-Noodle Soup

Take your choice—serve this tasty soup as a main dish for three or as a side dish for six.

2 14½-ounce cans chicken
  broth
1 tablespoon soy sauce
1 tablespoon lemon juice
  Dash ground ginger
2 cups loose-pack frozen
  mixed broccoli, carrots,
  and onions
½ ounce (⅓ cup) packaged
  medium egg noodles
1½ cups chopped cooked
  chicken

● In a large saucepan combine chicken broth, soy sauce, lemon juice, and ginger. Bring to boiling, then add frozen vegetables and noodles. Return to boiling, then reduce heat. Cover and simmer for 7 minutes.

● Add chicken. Return to boiling again, then reduce heat. Cover and simmer about 1 minute more or till vegetables are tender and noodles are al dente (tender but still firm). Serves 3.

Seafood Primavera

1 5-ounce package corkscrew
  macaroni with vegetables
  and cream sauce *or* one
  4½-ounce package
  noodles with Parmesan
  cheese sauce
1½ cups loose-pack frozen
  mixed zucchini, carrots,
  cauliflower, lima beans,
  and Italian beans, *or*
  frozen mixed cauliflower,
  broccoli, and carrots
½ teaspoon dried basil,
  crushed
1 8-ounce package frozen
  peeled and deveined
  shrimp *or* 8 ounces crab-
  flavored fish sticks
1 3-ounce package cream
  cheese
1 medium tomato

● Cook pasta mix according to package directions, *except* add frozen mixed vegetables and basil to the boiling water with the pasta mix. If using frozen shrimp, add them to mixture the last 2 minutes of cooking.

● Meanwhile, if using crab-flavored fish sticks, cut them into 1-inch pieces. Cut the cream cheese into cubes. Cut the tomato into wedges.

● If using fish sticks, add pieces to pasta mixture. Then add cream cheese to the pasta mixture. Cook, covered, over low heat about 2 minutes more or till cream cheese is melted and fish is heated through.

● To serve, spoon mixture onto dinner plates and garnish with tomato wedges. Makes 3 servings.

Swiss-Sauced Tortellini with Asparagus

There is a difference—fresh and frozen tortellini cook faster than dried.

1 7-ounce package cheese-filled tortellini (not dried)
1 8- *or* 10-ounce package frozen cut asparagus
2 tablespoons margarine *or* butter
2 tablespoons all-purpose flour
⅛ teaspoon ground nutmeg
1 cup milk
1 4-ounce can sliced mushrooms, drained
1 2-ounce jar diced pimiento, drained
4 ounces sliced process Swiss cheese, torn into pieces

● Cook tortellini according to package directions, *except* add frozen asparagus the last 3 to 5 minutes of cooking. Drain.

● Meanwhile, for sauce, in a medium saucepan melt margarine or butter. Stir in flour and nutmeg. Add milk. Cook and stir till thickened and bubbly. Then cook and stir for 1 minute more. Add mushrooms, pimiento, and Swiss cheese. Cook and stir just till cheese is melted.

● To serve, pour cheese sauce over hot tortellini and asparagus. Gently toss till coated. Transfer to a serving dish. Serves 4.

To micro-cook: Cook tortellini and asparagus as above.
● For sauce, in a medium microwave-safe bowl place margarine or butter. Micro-cook, uncovered, on 100% power (high) for 45 to 60 seconds or till melted. Stir in flour and nutmeg. Add milk. Cook, uncovered, on high for 3 to 5 minutes or till thickened, stirring after every minute. Stir in mushrooms, pimiento, and cheese. Cook, uncovered, on high for 1 to 1½ minutes more or till cheese is melted, stirring after 45 seconds. Serve as above.

Italian Tortellini Salad

Team pasta with crispy greens as the base for a great one-dish meal.

2 cups loose-pack frozen mixed broccoli, carrots, and cauliflower, *or* one 9-ounce package frozen artichoke hearts
4 ounces provolone cheese *or* mozzarella cheese
1 2¼-ounce can sliced pitted ripe olives, drained
4 cups torn mixed salad greens
1 pint (2 cups) deli marinated tortellini salad
1 3½-ounce package sliced pepperoni
¼ cup grated Parmesan cheese
   Clear Italian dressing (optional)

● Place frozen vegetables in a colander. Run *hot water* over vegetables just till thawed. Drain vegetables well. Cut provolone or mozzarella cheese into ½-inch cubes.

● For salad, in a large salad bowl combine drained vegetables, cheese cubes, olives, salad greens, *undrained* tortellini salad, pepperoni slices, and Parmesan cheese. Gently toss till coated. If necessary, add enough of the Italian dressing to coat. If desired, sprinkle with additional Parmesan cheese. Makes 4 servings.

Off-the-Shelf Italian Dinner

Off-the-Shelf Italian Dinner

Use half green and half plain tortellini for a colorful dish. (Pictured at left and on the cover.)

12 ounces package cheese-
    filled tortellini (not dried)
1 tablespoon snipped parsley
1 10½-ounce can ready-to-
    serve low-sodium tomato
    soup with tomato pieces
½ of a 6-ounce can (⅓ cup)
    tomato paste
½ teaspoon dried marjoram,
    crushed
    Dash bottled hot pepper
    sauce
1 6½-ounce can minced clams
    Finely shredded *or* grated
    Parmesan cheese

● Cook tortellini in boiling unsalted water according to package directions. Drain in a colander, then transfer to a warm serving dish. Add parsley. Gently toss.

● Meanwhile, for clam sauce, in another saucepan stir together soup, tomato paste, marjoram, and hot pepper sauce. Cook till bubbly. Add *undrained* clams, then heat through.

● To serve, spoon hot clam mixture over hot tortellini. Sprinkle with Parmesan cheese. Makes 4 servings.

To micro-cook: Cook tortellini as above. Then toss the tortellini with parsley.
● Meanwhile, for sauce, in a 1-quart microwave-safe casserole stir together soup, tomato paste, marjoram, and hot pepper sauce. Micro-cook, covered, on 100% power (high) for 3 to 4 minutes or till bubbly, stirring after 2 minutes. Stir in *undrained* clams. Micro-cook, covered, on high for 2 to 3 minutes more or till heated through. Serve as above.

Chili Spaghetti Ring

1 8-ounce package American-
    style spaghetti dinner mix
2 tablespoons margarine
    or butter
1 cup (4 ounces) shredded
    Monterey Jack cheese
¼ cup snipped parsley
1 15½-ounce can small red
    beans, drained
1 15-ounce can tomato sauce
    with tomato tidbits
1 teaspoon chili powder
    Pepper
½ cup unsalted peanuts
    Parsley sprigs

● Cook the spaghetti from dinner mix according to package directions. Drain spaghetti in a colander.

● In a mixing bowl combine cooked spaghetti, margarine or butter, the sauce mix from the dinner mix, Monterey Jack cheese, and parsley. Gently toss till well combined. Press mixture into an oiled 3½- or 4-cup ring mold. Let stand 5 minutes.

● Meanwhile, for sauce, in saucepan combine beans, tomato sauce, and chili powder. Bring to boiling. Reduce heat. Simmer, uncovered, for 5 minutes. Season to taste with pepper.

● To serve, unmold spaghetti onto serving platter. Pour sauce in center of the spaghetti ring. Then sprinkle with peanuts. If desired, garnish with parsley sprigs. Makes 4 or 5 servings.

Vegetable Salad Shells

Serve this marinated salad with grilled burgers for an easy summertime meal.

1 10-ounce package frozen
   mixed vegetables *or* one
   16-ounce can mixed
   vegetables
⅓ cup vinegar
¼ cup salad oil
2 tablespoons sugar
2 tablespoons finely chopped
   onion
2 tablespoons finely chopped
   green pepper
½ teaspoon celery seed
½ teaspoon mustard seed
   Several dashes bottled hot
   pepper sauce
12 jumbo pasta shells
   (conchiglioni)
6 small lettuce leaves

● If using frozen vegetables, cook them according to package directions, then drain. Or, drain canned vegetables.

● In a mixing bowl stir together vinegar, oil, sugar, onion, green pepper, celery seed, mustard seed, and hot pepper sauce. Stir in cooked vegetables. Then cover and chill for at least 4 hours.

● Cook pasta as directed on page 10. Drain in a colander. Then cover and chill.

● To serve, use a slotted spoon to spoon vegetable mixture into pasta shells. Line 6 salad plates with lettuce. For each serving, arrange *2* stuffed shells onto *each* plate. Makes 6 servings.

Vegetable-Couscous Pilaf

When sweet red peppers aren't available, use sweet yellow or green bell peppers instead.

¾ cup chicken *or* beef broth
1 medium carrot, sliced
   (½ cup)
½ of a small zucchini, thinly
   sliced (½ cup)
½ of a medium sweet red
   pepper, chopped (¼ cup)
1 2½-ounce jar sliced
   mushrooms, drained
1 clove garlic, minced,
   or ⅛ teaspoon garlic
   powder
½ teaspoon dried oregano,
   crushed
¼ teaspoon salt
½ cup quick-cooking couscous

● In a medium saucepan stir together chicken or beef broth, carrot, zucchini, sweet red pepper, mushrooms, garlic, oregano, and salt. Bring to boiling. Reduce heat. Then cover and simmer for 3 minutes.

● Remove saucepan from heat. Stir in couscous. Then let stand, covered, about 5 minutes or till liquid is absorbed. Using a fork, fluff mixture before serving. Makes 4 servings.

Vegetable Salad Shells

Pasta with Parsley Pesto

For easy measuring, snip the fresh parsley with kitchen shears in a measuring cup.

8 ounces spaghetti
    or other packaged pasta
1½ cups snipped parsley
⅓ cup grated Parmesan
    or Romano cheese
¼ cup toasted walnuts
2 teaspoons dried basil,
    crushed
2 cloves garlic, quartered
3 tablespoons olive oil
    or cooking oil
    Cracked pepper
    Grated Parmesan
    or Romano cheese

● Cook pasta as directed on page 10. Drain pasta in a colander then transfer to a warm serving dish. If necessary, cover pasta to keep warm.

● Meanwhile, for pesto, in a blender container or food processor bowl combine parsley, ⅓ cup cheese, walnuts, basil, and garlic. Cover and blend or process till a paste forms. (When necessary, stop and scrape sides.) With lid ajar, gradually add oil, blending or processing till smooth, stopping to scrape mixture down from sides as needed.

● Spoon *half* (about ⅓ cup) of the pesto on top of the hot cooked pasta. (Refrigerate or freeze remaining pesto for another time.) Then gently toss pasta till coated with pesto. Sprinkle with cracked pepper and additional cheese. Serve immediately. Makes 8 servings.

Creamy Noodles 'n' Vegetables

It's easy to make cheese-sauced side dishes when you use a purchased soft cheese product.

5 ounces packaged medium-
    size, curly-edge noodles
    (mafalda) *or* linguine
1 10-ounce package frozen
    mixed vegetables *or*
    cut broccoli
½ of an 8-ounce container of
    soft-style cream cheese
    with chives and onion
¼ cup milk
    Salt
    Pepper

● Cook the pasta as directed on page 10, *except* add frozen vegetables the last 3 to 5 minutes of cooking. Drain pasta vegetable mixture in a colander, then return mixture to the saucepan.

● Add cream cheese and milk. Cook and stir till cream cheese is melted and mixture is heated through. Season to taste with salt and pepper. Makes 4 servings.

Vegetable-Bordered Pasta Bake

Broccoli flowerets make an impressive border for this picnic or party take-along.

 4 ounces packaged whole wheat spaghetti *or* packaged fettuccine
 1 10-ounce package frozen chopped broccoli
 ½ cup chopped onion
 ¼ cup chopped green *or* sweet red pepper
 1 clove garlic, minced
 1 tablespoon margarine *or* butter
 1 tablespoon cornstarch
 1 cup milk
 ¾ cup shredded American cheese (3 ounces)
 1 8-ounce can water chestnuts, drained and coarsely chopped
 2 cups desired cooked vegetables

● Break pasta into 1-inch pieces. Cook pasta as directed on page 10. Drain in a colander.

● Meanwhile, in a covered saucepan, cook broccoli, onion, green or sweet red pepper, and garlic in a small amount of water about 10 minutes or till broccoli is nearly tender. Drain.

● For sauce, in a small saucepan melt margarine or butter. Stir in cornstarch, ¼ teaspoon *salt,* and ⅛ teaspoon *pepper.* Add milk. Cook and stir till thickened and bubbly. Then cook and stir 2 minutes more. Add cheese. Cook and stir just till melted.

● Gently stir together pasta, sauce, broccoli mixture, and water chestnuts. Transfer to a 10x6x2-inch baking dish. Arrange desired cooked vegetables around the dish. Cover and bake in a 350° oven about 30 minutes or until heated through. Serves 6.

Assembling the casserole
Transfer the pasta mixture to the baking dish, then arrange the desired cooked vegetables around the outside edge of the mixture.

Vegetable borders are an easy way to dress up almost any casserole.

Creamy Pasta and
Cabbage Salad

Creamy Pasta and Cabbage Salad

Look in the produce department for a mixture of preshredded cabbage and carrots, or shred your own.

1½ cups corkscrew macaroni
    (rotelle)
½ cup plain yogurt
⅓ cup creamy Italian salad
    dressing
1 tablespoon grated
    Parmesan cheese
1 small clove garlic, minced
2 cups mixed shredded
    cabbage and carrots
1 medium cucumber,
    chopped
1 medium tomato, seeded
    and chopped
    Milk
    Lettuce leaves (optional)

● Cook pasta as directed on page 10. Drain in a colander. Rinse with cold water, then drain again.

● Meanwhile, for dressing, in a small bowl stir together yogurt, Italian salad dressing, Parmesan cheese, and garlic.

● In a large salad bowl combine pasta, shredded cabbage and carrots, cucumber, and tomato. Pour dressing over the pasta mixture. Gently toss till coated. Cover and chill for 2 to 8 hours.

● To serve: if necessary, stir in a few tablespoons of milk to moisten mixture. If desired, serve salad on top of lettuce leaves. Makes 6 servings.

Lemon-Fresh Waldorf Salad

A perfect picnic salad—easy to make and easy to tote.

1 cup wagon wheel macaroni
    (ruote) *or* tiny pasta bows
    (tripolini)
¾ cup chopped celery
¼ cup raisins
3 small apples, cored and
    chopped
½ cup mayonnaise *or* salad
    dressing
½ cup lemon yogurt
2 tablespoons sunflower nuts

● Cook pasta as directed on page 10. Drain in a colander. Rinse with cold water, then drain again. Cover and chill.

● In a large plastic container with a sealable lid combine chilled pasta, chopped celery, and raisins.

● For dressing, in a medium bowl stir together the chopped apples, mayonnaise or salad dressing, and yogurt. Spread the mayonnaise mixture over the pasta mixture. Sprinkle with the sunflower nuts. Cover and chill for at least 4 hours.

● Transport the salad in an insulated cooler with an ice pack. To serve, fold dressing into pasta mixture. Serves 8 to 10.

Chinese Egg Rolls

8 dried mushrooms
1 whole medium chicken
    breast (about 12 ounces),
    skinned and boned
1 tablespoon rice wine
    or dry sherry
1 tablespoon cooking oil
2 teaspoons grated gingerroot
2 cups fresh bean sprouts
2 medium carrots, shredded
4 green onions, thinly sliced
1 teaspoon sugar
1 teaspoon sesame oil
    (optional)
¼ teaspoon salt
10 packaged egg roll wrappers
    Cooking oil for deep-fat
    frying
    Bottled sweet-and-sour
    sauce *or* mustard sauce
    (optional)

● In a small mixing bowl soak mushrooms in enough *hot water* to cover for 30 minutes. Rinse well and squeeze to remove excess water. Discard stems. Then finely chop mushrooms.

● Cut chicken into thin strips, then cut strips into matchstick-size shreds. Transfer chicken to a mixing bowl, then sprinkle with rice wine or dry sherry.

● For filling, preheat a wok or large skillet over high heat. Add 1 tablespoon cooking oil. (Add more oil as necessary during cooking.) Cook and stir gingerroot in hot oil for 15 seconds. Add chicken, then cook and stir for 1½ minutes. Add bean sprouts, carrots, green onions, and mushrooms. Cook and stir for 2 minutes or till chicken is tender and vegetables are nearly tender. Stir in sugar, sesame oil (if desired), and salt. Then remove from heat and cool filling before assembling egg rolls.

● To assemble egg rolls, for *each* egg roll, position an egg roll wrapper with 1 point toward you. Spoon about ⅓ *cup* of the cool filling diagonally across the skin, just below the center. Fold bottom point over filling, tucking point under the filling. Then fold the side corners toward the center and roll up. Moisten the top point with water, then press to seal. Repeat with remaining egg roll wrappers and filling mixture.

● In a wok, 2-quart saucepan, or deep-fat fryer, heat 1½ to 2 inches of cooking oil to 365°. Fry egg rolls, 2 or 3 at a time, in the hot oil for 2 to 4 minutes or till golden brown, turning once. Remove from oil. Drain on paper towels. Keep warm in a 300° oven while frying remaining egg rolls. If desired, serve with sweet-and-sour or hot mustard sauce. Makes 10.

Pop-the-Cork Pasta Crunch

1 7-ounce package corkscrew
    macaroni (rotelle)
½ cup grated Parmesan cheese
½ teaspoon Italian seasoning
⅛ teaspoon garlic salt
    Cooking oil for deep-fat
    frying

● Cook pasta as directed on page 10. Drain in a colander. Rinse with cold water, then drain again. Pat excess moisture from pasta with paper towels. In a small mixing bowl stir together Parmesan cheese, Italian seasoning, and garlic salt; set aside.

● In a deep skillet or deep-fat fryer heat 1½ inches of cooking oil to 365°. Fry pasta, a slotted spoonful at a time, in the hot oil for 1 to 2 minutes or till lightly browned, stirring to separate. Using the slotted spoon, remove pasta from oil. Drain on paper towels. While macaroni is warm, sprinkle with the cheese mixture. Gently toss till coated. Cool. Makes 10 (½-cup) servings.

Sweet Snacks

Pack this crunchy snack in a decorative container for holiday gift-giving.

8 ounces fusilli (twisted spaghetti), broken into 2-inch pieces, *or* tiny pasta bows (tripolini)	● Cook pasta as directed on page 10. Drain in a colander. Rinse with cold water, then drain again. Pat excess moisture from pasta with paper towels.

8 ounces fusilli (twisted spaghetti), broken into 2-inch pieces, *or* tiny pasta bows (tripolini)
   Cooking oil for deep-fat frying
½ cup chopped pecans
¾ cup sugar
⅓ cup margarine *or* butter
3 tablespoons light corn syrup
¼ teaspoon baking soda
1 teaspoon vanilla

● Cook pasta as directed on page 10. Drain in a colander. Rinse with cold water, then drain again. Pat excess moisture from pasta with paper towels.

● In a deep skillet or deep-fat fryer heat 1½ inches of cooking oil to 365°. Fry pasta, a slotted spoonful at a time, in the hot oil for 1 to 2 minutes or till lightly browned, stirring to separate. Using the slotted spoon, remove pasta from oil. Drain on paper towels. Then transfer pasta to a buttered 17x12x2-inch baking pan. Sprinkle with nuts. Set pasta and nuts aside.

● In a 1-quart saucepan combine sugar, margarine or butter, and corn syrup. Cook and stir over medium heat till sugar dissolves and mixture comes to boiling. Then boil at a moderately steady rate over entire surface about 5 minutes (or to 255°), stirring occasionally. Remove from heat. Stir in soda. Then stir in vanilla. Immediately pour syrup mixture over pasta and nuts. Mix well. Spread mixture in single layer in the pan.

● Bake in a 300° oven for 15 minutes. Stir. Then bake in the 300° oven for 5 minutes more. Transfer pasta and nuts to a piece of buttered foil. Cool. Makes about 5 (½-cup) servings.

Sweet Noodle Kugel

For fewer servings, cut the recipe in half and bake it in an 8x8x2-inch baking pan.

1 16-ounce package wide egg noodles
1 24-ounce carton cream-style cottage cheese
3 apples, peeled, cored, and sliced (about 2¾ cups)
¼ cups raisins
1 8-ounce can crushed pineapple (juice pack)
1 cup sugar
1 tablespoon ground cinnamon
2 tablespoons margarine *or* butter, melted
   Sliced apples

● Cook egg noodles according to package direction. Drain in a colander, then set aside. In a large mixing bowl stir together cottage cheese, 2¾ cups sliced apples, raisins, and *undrained* pineapple. In a small bowl stir together sugar and cinnamon.

● In a greased 13x9x2-inch baking dish place *one-third* of the cooked and drained noodles. Top with *half* of the cottage cheese mixture and *one-third* of the sugar-cinnamon mixture. Place another one-third of the noodles on top, add the remaining cottage cheese mixture, and sprinkle with another third of the sugar-cinnamon. End layering with the last of the noodles.

● Brush margarine or butter over top layer of noodles. Then sprinkle with remaining sugar-cinnamon mixture. Arrange the additional sliced apples on top in the center. Cover with foil. Bake in a 325° oven about 1 hour or till hot and apples are tender. Serve kugel immediately, spooning juices from bottom of baking dish over each serving. Makes 12 to 15 servings.

Index

Have BETTER HOMES AND GAR
magazine delivered to your
For information, write to:
MR. ROBERT AUSTIN
P.O. BOX 4536
DES MOINES, IA 50336